TABLE OF CONTENTS

1 — The Heart of a Leader
Explore how humility and a servant's heart are foundational to effective, Christ-centered leadership.

2 — The Team of a Leader
Learn to lead a team boldly by stepping into challenges and serving others with selflessness and grace.

3 — The Accountability of a Leader
Understand the importance of accountability and how it fosters growth, trust, and integrity in leadership.

4 — The Habits of a Leader
Discover how intentional habits and disciplined routines create a strong foundation for leadership success.

5 — Leading with Openness & Boldness
Uncover the power of vulnerability and honesty to build trust and inspire those you lead.

6 — Great Leaders Lead Themselves
Learn practical ways to manage yourself—emotionally, spiritually, and physically—to lead others effectively.

Introduction

The Call to Lead Like Jesus

Have you ever wondered who can be a leader or what truly makes someone a great leader? Maybe you've asked yourself the simplest yet most profound question: What is a leader?

At their core, a leader is someone who has a vision—a picture of what could be—and the direction to inspire and guide others toward it. Great leaders motivate people, helping them see possibilities they might never have imagined for themselves. They encourage ordinary individuals to achieve extraordinary results, all while nurturing the next generation of leaders.

As Christians, we have the privilege and the challenge of following the greatest leader of all time—Jesus Christ. His life wasn't just an example; it was a masterclass in leadership. Every follower of Jesus is called to lead in some capacity. Whether it's within your family, your workplace, your community, or even your church, the call to leadership is woven into our faith.

In this book, we'll take a close, practical look at the life of Jesus—His actions, His words, and His heart for others. We'll learn from the ultimate leader how to lead with wisdom, humility, and grace in a world that desperately needs these qualities.

Introduction

What Is Leadership?

Here's the thing: leadership isn't a position, a title, or a spot on an organizational chart. Leadership is influence—pure and simple. It's the ability to affect others' actions, thoughts, and lives, whether you realize it or not.

Think about it: a mom who teaches her children the value of kindness, a teacher who encourages a struggling student to keep going, a friend who offers guidance during a tough time—all of these are leaders. Leadership doesn't require a stage, a microphone, or an audience of thousands. It requires a heart willing to serve and the courage to step into the gap where influence is needed.

Some people hold positions of authority but lack the trust and love of those they lead. Others, without titles or official power, are deeply respected because they genuinely care for and support others. True leadership isn't about rank or recognition—it's about relationships. It's about trust, care, and genuine connection.

Leadership Misunderstood

Too often, leadership is tied to status or achievements, but that's not where its power lies. I've seen people with impressive titles who failed to inspire those around them. Their teams followed instructions out of obligation or fear, but there was no trust, no loyalty, and no growth.

Introduction

On the other hand, I've seen individuals in the quietest corners of an organization, holding no title, who were the ones people turned to in moments of crisis or confusion. These unsung leaders didn't need authority to make a difference—they led through kindness, integrity, and a genuine desire to help others succeed.

The Heart of a Great Leader

A great leader isn't obsessed with being the star of the show. They're more interested in raising others up, helping them shine, and celebrating their successes. They prioritize serving the needs of others over their own ambitions. They give credit when things go well and take responsibility when they don't.

This kind of leadership reflects the heart of Jesus. Throughout His ministry, Jesus wasn't concerned with gaining fame or recognition. He was focused on loving people, healing the broken, and empowering His disciples to carry on His mission. His leadership was rooted in humility, service, and a deep understanding of people's needs.

Why Leadership Matters

God has uniquely equipped you to lead, even if you feel unqualified. He knows your strengths and weaknesses and has designed you for a purpose. He's not surprised by your passions or the things that light up your soul. In fact, He wants to use those very things to accomplish His plans through you.

Introduction

Studies show that people prefer to follow leaders who are authentic over those who are always "right." Authenticity builds trust, and trust is the foundation of great leadership. Unfortunately, poor leadership has caused many people to walk away from churches, organizations, and even relationships.

In many cases, it's not the church or organization itself that people dislike—it's the leadership. When leaders fail to create an environment where people feel valued, supported, and empowered, they unintentionally drive others away.

This book is about changing that. It's about becoming the kind of leader who inspires others to grow and thrive. It's about learning from Jesus—the ultimate model of leadership—and applying His lessons in your own life.

Introduction

The Journey Ahead

Whether you're leading your family, a small group, or a large organization, you have the opportunity to lead like Jesus. This book isn't just a guide; it's an invitation. It's an invitation to step into the leader God created you to be—a leader who influences with love, serves with humility, and builds a legacy of trust and transformation. A shepherd's guide. Whether shepherding your children, church, or employees, utilize and apply these lessons in your context.

So, as we embark on this journey together, I want you to remember: as long as you have breath in your lungs, you're called to lead. Let's learn from the greatest leader who ever lived and become the leaders our world so desperately needs.

In this book, we will cover the following topics in the upcoming chapters:

1 The Heart of the Leader
2 The Team of the Leader
3 The Accountability of the Leader
4 The Habits of a Leader
5 Leading with Openness and Boldness
6 Great Leaders Lead Themselves

CHAPTER 1

THE HEART OF THE LEADER

1. THE HEART OF THE LEADER

Every leader leaves a mark, but the nature of that mark—the legacy—depends entirely on the heart of the leader. Leadership is not simply about skills, strategies, or charisma; it's about the condition of your heart. That's why the Bible urges us, *"Above all else, guard your heart, for everything you do flows from it"* (Proverbs 4:23).

Your heart is the wellspring of your life. Your actions, decisions, and motives are all shaped by the state of your heart. If your heart is aligned with God's purposes, your leadership will naturally reflect His character. But if your heart is misaligned—driven by pride, fear, or selfish ambition—your leadership will veer off course, no matter how well-intentioned you may be.

Guarding the Heart

Guarding your heart is not a one-time action; it's a lifelong practice. Why? Because the enemy is constantly seeking ways to infiltrate it. If he succeeds, your motives shift, your focus blurs, and your leadership becomes about something other than serving others and glorifying God.

King David understood this vulnerability well. That's why he prayed, *"Search me, God, and know my heart; test me and know my anxious thoughts. See if there is any offensive way in me, and lead me in the way everlasting"* (Psalm 139:23-24). David wasn't afraid to ask God for a heart check because he knew the consequences of leading from an unexamined heart.

1. THE HEART OF THE LEADER

As leaders, we must regularly pause and reflect on the state of our hearts.

Ask yourself:
- Why am I doing what I'm doing?
- Are my motives rooted in service or self-interest?
- Am I staying aligned with God's vision for my life and leadership?
- Have I allowed pride or fear to creep in?

The "Why" of Leadership

Most leadership books focus on what to do and how to do it. While these are important, they miss the most critical question: Why are you doing it?

Your "why" reveals the true motive behind your leadership. If your "why" is driven by self-promotion, recognition, or control, your leadership will ultimately serve yourself rather than others. But if your "why" is rooted in obedience to God and a desire to serve others, your leadership will be transformational.

It's easy to drift from your original "why," which is why accountability is essential. Surround yourself with people who will lovingly challenge you to stay true to your calling and keep your heart aligned with God's purpose.

1. THE HEART OF THE LEADER

Self-Centered vs. Servant Leadership

There are two types of leaders: self-centered leaders and servant leaders.

- Self-Centered Leaders lead for personal gain. They crave titles, positions, and power. They want to be admired, served, and respected. Their leadership revolves around their needs, ambitions, and reputation.

- Servant Leaders, on the other hand, lead out of a deep sense of calling. Their focus is not on themselves but on the people they serve. They embody humility, prioritizing the needs of others above their own.

Self-Centered Leaders	Servant Leader
Very insecure and afraid of allowing others to take leadership roles and potentially exceed them.	Possess strong self-confidence, which allows them to focus on drawing out the best in others.
Want to be the only ones in the spotlight, unwilling to let anyone else take the lead.	Love to see others shine, nurture new talents, and encourage young leaders to step up and take the lead.
Avoid competition and ensure that everyone remains beneath them.	Empower others by creating opportunities for them to grow into leadership roles and take on greater responsibilities.
Seek to create the impression that they are great.	Work hard to make others feel great.
Seek approval based on their performance and that of others.	Seek God's approval.
Their actions instill fear in others.	Inspire others to build confidence.
Look for someone to blame.	Usually take responsibility.
Demand loyalty.	Extend grace and build trust.
Like and need to control people.	Like to empower people.
They are often guarded.	They are usually transparent.

1. THE HEART OF THE LEADER

Jesus is the ultimate example of a servant leader. He came not to be served but to serve, and His leadership changed the world forever. As Paul wrote in Philippians 2:7-9, Jesus humbled Himself, taking on the nature of a servant. And because He served, He was exalted.

When you lead like Jesus—putting others first and serving with humility—your leadership becomes a reflection of God's heart.

"Not so with you"

One of the most striking lessons on leadership in Scripture is found in Matthew 20. A mother, advocating for her sons, asks Jesus to grant them positions of prominence in His Kingdom. She wants them to sit at His right and left, symbolic of earthly power and prestige.

The other disciples are indignant—not because they disagree with her, but probably because they wish they'd thought to ask first. Their reactions reveal a heart condition that many leaders struggle with: the desire for status over service.

Jesus responds with a radical statement: *"Not so with you"* (Matthew 20:26). He contrasts worldly leadership—marked by authority, control, and self-interest—with godly leadership, which is rooted in service and humility.

LEADERSHIP

1. THE HEART OF THE LEADER

"Whoever wants to become great among you must be your servant, and whoever wants to be first must be your slave—just as the Son of Man did not come to be served, but to serve, and to give His life as a ransom for many" (Matthew 20:26-28).

In these few words, Jesus redefines greatness. True leadership isn't about being served; it's about serving others.

Servant Leadership in Action

To serve like Jesus means putting others' needs ahead of your own. It means leading with humility and a willingness to sacrifice. It's not about recognition or reward—it's about obedience to God and love for others.

Think about the people who have impacted your life the most. Chances are, they weren't the most powerful or successful by the world's standards. They were the ones who served you, believed in you, and invested in you when you needed it most.

Maybe it was a parent who worked tirelessly to provide for you, a teacher who saw potential in you, or a mentor who gave you opportunities when no one else would. Their influence came from their willingness to serve, not their desire to be celebrated.

As leaders, we have the same opportunity to impact others by serving them well.

1. THE HEART OF THE LEADER

The Pitfalls of Pride and Fear

Two of the greatest threats to servant leadership are pride and fear.

- *Pride makes leadership about you. It leads to self-reliance, arrogance, and a lack of empathy for others. Pride blinds you to your weaknesses and prevents you from seeking God's guidance.*

- *Fear creates insecurity and defensiveness. It makes you focus on protecting yourself rather than serving others. Fear can lead to trust issues—not only with others but also with God.*

Both pride and fear pull your heart away from God and hinder your ability to lead like Jesus. The antidote is humility: *"Learn from me, for I am gentle and humble in heart"* (Matthew 11:29). Humility keeps your heart aligned with God and your leadership focused on serving others.

A Changed Heart Equals a Changed Leader

If you've recognized self-centered tendencies in your leadership, don't be discouraged. Change begins with the heart. When you allow God to transform your heart, your leadership will naturally follow.

Put God first. Trust Him as your provider and guide. Seek His approval above all else. When your heart is aligned with His, you'll lead with authenticity, humility, and purpose.

1. THE HEART OF THE LEADER

Reflection Questions:

What's one specific way you can start serving others on a regular basis?

Think of a leader who has impacted your life—what did they do that made a difference?

1. THE HEART OF THE LEADER

Reflection Questions:

In what areas of your leadership do you need to guard your heart more closely?

Are there any areas where pride or fear have crept in? How can you surrender those to God?

CHAPTER 2

THE TEAM OF A LEADER

2. THE TEAM OF THE LEADER

One of the most dangerous lies a leader can tell themselves is, "I can do it better on my own." It's an alluring thought that whispers pride and self-reliance into the heart, but the truth is, no one achieves greatness alone. Whether you're leading a ministry, a family, or a business, the most important tool in your leadership toolkit isn't your talent or your vision—it's your team.

The Bible gives us a clear picture of how God designed leadership: it's not a solo endeavor. Even Jesus, who could have done everything perfectly on His own, chose to work with a team. If the greatest leader of all time saw the value in collaboration, how much more should we?

The Importance of a Team

Think of a sports team. A star player may shine, but a lone athlete cannot win the game. Each member has a role, and the success of the team hinges on everyone playing their part. In leadership, it's the same.

Jesus understood this profoundly. From the very beginning of His ministry, His first priority was building a team. He didn't need a team—He was God incarnate, fully capable of working miracles and changing hearts single-handedly. Yet, He chose to surround Himself with people and pour His life into them. Why? Because Jesus wasn't just focused on His immediate mission; He was preparing a group to carry on His work after He returned to the Father.

2. THE TEAM OF A LEADER

Jesus didn't just pick anyone, though. He chose strategically and prayerfully. Luke 6:12 tells us that Jesus spent an entire night in prayer before selecting His twelve apostles. This was the only time recorded in Scripture where Jesus prayed all night, underscoring how critical this decision was.

Choosing the Right Team

How do you pick the right people for your team? It's tempting to choose based on proximity, convenience, or even qualifications. But Jesus modeled something deeper—He looked for people who were teachable, humble, and committed.

Interestingly, when we look at Jesus' team, it wasn't filled with the most obviously talented or experienced individuals. Peter was an impulsive fisherman. Matthew was a tax collector—someone hated and mistrusted by society. Simon the Zealot was a political radical. None of them seemed like ideal candidates for transforming the world.

Yet Jesus wasn't looking for perfection; He was looking for potential. He chose people He could shape, train, and empower. Their willingness to follow and their hearts for the mission mattered more than their résumés.

© EgyptProject.org

2. THE TEAM OF A LEADER

Investing in Your Team

Having a team isn't enough. What sets great leaders apart is their willingness to invest in their team. Jesus spent three years pouring into His disciples. He taught them, challenged them, corrected them, and, most importantly, empowered them.

In Matthew 10:1, we see Jesus giving His disciples authority—the right to make decisions and act in His name. This wasn't just delegation; it was empowerment. By giving them authority, He showed that He trusted them, even though He knew they would sometimes fail.

As leaders, we must do the same. Empower your team to take ownership of their roles. Allow them to grow through their mistakes, and always provide a safe space for them to learn and improve.

The Power of Trust and Communication

Trust is the foundation of any strong team. Without it, even the most talented group will crumble under pressure. Trust isn't given blindly, though; it's built over time through consistent actions.

Think of trust like a bank account. Every time you show integrity, keep your word, or support your team, you're making a deposit. Every time you let them down or micromanage, you're making a withdrawal. Run out of trust, and your team will stop believing in your leadership.

2. THE TEAM OF A LEADER

Communication is another cornerstone of effective teamwork. Jesus communicated His mission clearly to His disciples. He didn't leave them guessing about their purpose or their role in His vision. As leaders, we must do the same. A team without clear communication is like a ship without a rudder—it will drift aimlessly.

The Servant Leader's Team

Jesus' leadership was rooted in service, and He called His team to lead in the same way. In John 13, we see Jesus washing His disciples' feet—a task reserved for the lowest servant. He then told them, *"I have set you an example that you should do as I have done for you"* (John 13:15).

A servant leader prioritizes their team's growth and well-being over their own comfort or agenda. They lead by example, showing humility, grace, and a willingness to do whatever it takes to support the mission.

2. THE TEAM OF A LEADER

Practical Steps for Building a Godly Team

- **Pray First:** *Follow Jesus' example and pray before making decisions about your team. Ask God to guide you to the right people.*

- **Look Beyond Talent:** *Choose team members based on their character, heart, and teachability, not just their skills or experience.*

- **Empower Your Team:** *Give your team authority and trust them to make decisions. Be there to support and guide them, but don't micromanage.*

- **Communicate Clearly:** *Share the vision and goals with your team regularly. Make sure everyone understands their role in achieving the mission.*

- **Invest in Relationships:** *Spend time getting to know your team members. Build trust by being approachable, transparent, and supportive.*

2. THE TEAM OF A LEADER

Conclusion

No leader succeeds alone. Even Jesus, the Son of God, chose to work with a team. As leaders, we must embrace the same model—building, investing in, and empowering the people God places around us.

Your team is not just a resource; they are your ministry. When you pour into them, you're not just building a stronger organization—you're building people who can impact the world for Christ.

2. THE TEAM OF A LEADER

Reflection Questions:

Think of a time when you tried to handle everything on your own. What did you learn from that experience?

Have you been prayerfully considering the team around you, or have you relied on convenience to fill roles?

2. THE TEAM OF A LEADER

Reflection Questions:

Are there areas in your leadership where you've struggled to trust your team? How can you begin to build that trust?

Who in your team needs more investment, encouragement, or empowerment from you? How can you ensure your team is aligned with the vision God has given you?

CHAPTER 3

THE ACCOUNTABILITY OF THE LEADER

3. THE ACCOUNTABILITY OF THE LEADER

Accountability inspires people to take ownership and responsibility for achieving goals and fulfilling visions. It's not a punitive measure, nor is it a sign of weakness. True accountability is the intentional decision to invite others into your journey—to refine you, challenge you, and encourage you as you pursue your calling.

Why Accountability Matters

Imagine you're living in the time of Jesus. You're an ordinary person with a small farm, working hard to grow your crops and sell them at the market. One day, you encounter two men—Nicodemus, an esteemed teacher of the law, respected for his wisdom and advanced in age, and Jesus, a young carpenter from Nazareth, relatively unknown but captivating in His words and presence.

Who would you trust with your eternity? Who would you follow, learn from, or make your role model?

The lesson is clear: accountability, wisdom, and leadership are not determined by age, status, or appearances. They're rooted in depth of character, purpose, and a commitment to truth. Jesus, though younger and less outwardly impressive than Nicodemus, drew people because His life was marked by integrity, wisdom, and submission to the Father's will.

Similarly, accountability isn't about finding someone older or more accomplished. It's about connecting with someone who can speak truth into your life, someone who will challenge and encourage you to be the best version of yourself in Christ.

3. THE ACCOUNTABILITY OF THE LEADER

What Accountability Is—and What It Isn't

Accountability is often misunderstood. Some view it as an opportunity for blame or judgment, but that couldn't be further from the truth. True accountability is rooted in love and mutual respect. It's about having someone who will walk with you through challenges, celebrate your victories, and hold you to the standards you've committed to.

Studies show that people are significantly more likely to achieve their goals when they share them with someone else. Why? Because accountability shifts your mindset from "I'll try" to "I will." When you know you'll need to check in with someone, you're more likely to follow through.

Think about your own experiences. Have you ever prepared for a doctor's visit by paying closer attention to your diet or exercise habits? Or flossed extra carefully before a dentist appointment? That's accountability in action. The knowledge that someone else will evaluate your progress motivates you to give your best effort.

In leadership, accountability can mean the difference between stagnation and growth. It's what transforms good intentions into real, measurable outcomes.

3. THE ACCOUNTABILITY OF THE LEADER

The Biblical Framework for Accountability

The Bible is rich with examples of accountability. Proverbs 27:17 reminds us, *"As iron sharpens iron, so one person sharpens another."* This verse highlights the mutual benefit of accountability—it's not a one-sided relationship but a dynamic exchange where both parties grow.

Jesus Himself demonstrated accountability throughout His earthly ministry. He was fully submitted to the will of the Father, often retreating to pray and seek guidance. In John 5:19, He said, *"Very truly I tell you, the Son can do nothing by Himself; He can do only what He sees His Father doing."*

Jesus also modeled accountability within His relationships. He invested deeply in His disciples, teaching them, correcting them, and empowering them to carry on His work. Even within His inner circle, He fostered an environment where questions could be asked, and truths could be spoken.

3. THE ACCOUNTABILITY OF THE LEADER

Practical Steps to Embrace Accountability

- **Find the Right Partner:** Accountability isn't about finding a perfect person; it's about finding the right person. Look for someone who shares your values, understands your vision, and isn't afraid to challenge you. This could be a mentor, a peer, or even someone you're leading, as long as they're committed to your growth.

- **Be Transparent:** Accountability only works if you're honest. It's tempting to present a polished version of yourself, but true growth requires vulnerability. Be open about your struggles, doubts, and areas where you need improvement.

- **Set Clear Goals:** Accountability thrives on clarity. Whether you're working on a ministry project, improving a skill, or deepening your faith, make your goals specific and actionable. Share these goals with your accountability partner and establish a plan for regular check-ins.

- **Create a Routine:** Regularity is key to effective accountability. Schedule consistent meetings with your accountability partner, whether weekly, biweekly, or monthly. Use this time to review progress, discuss challenges, and celebrate victories.

- **Be Willing to Listen:** Accountability isn't just about reporting your progress; it's about receiving feedback. Be open to constructive criticism and willing to adjust your course as needed. Remember, the goal isn't perfection—it's growth.

3. THE ACCOUNTABILITY OF THE LEADER

The Impact of Accountability on Leadership

As a leader, your accountability doesn't just benefit you—it impacts everyone you lead. When you model accountability, you create a culture where responsibility, honesty, and growth are valued. Your team will follow your example, fostering an environment of trust and collaboration.

Accountability also protects leaders from burnout and isolation. It's easy to feel the weight of leadership and believe you must carry it alone. But God never intended for us to lead in isolation. Ecclesiastes 4:9-10 reminds us, *"Two are better than one, because they have a good return for their labor: If either of them falls down, one can help the other up."*

Conclusion

Accountability isn't a burden; it's a gift. It's an opportunity to invite others into your journey, to refine your character, and to stay aligned with God's calling on your life. Whether you're a pastor, a parent, or a professional, accountability will help you stay grounded, focused, and faithful.

Remember, our ultimate accountability is to God. One day, we will stand before Him and give an account of our lives. By embracing accountability now—with others and with Him—we prepare ourselves for that moment.

3. THE ACCOUNTABILITY OF THE LEADER

Reflection Questions:

How have you experienced the benefits of accountability in your life or leadership?

Is there an area where you've been avoiding accountability? Why? Who in your life could serve as an accountability partner or mentor?

3. THE ACCOUNTABILITY OF THE LEADER

Reflection Questions:

How can you create a culture of accountability within your team or organization?

What steps can you take this week to invite accountability into your leadership journey?

CHAPTER 4

THE HABITS OF A LEADER

4. THE HABITS OF A LEADER

Your habits will determine the quality of your leadership. They are the silent architects of your future, shaping your character, guiding your decisions, and ultimately influencing those you lead. Developing good habits doesn't just happen by accident; it requires intentionality, discipline, and consistency. If we change our habits, we can transform our leadership.

The Power of Habits in Leadership

Habits are more than just routines—they are the foundation of who we are becoming. Consider something as simple as brushing your teeth. This small, daily act leads to healthier teeth and a confident smile. Now, imagine the cumulative impact of a daily habit like reading Scripture or practicing gratitude. These habits deepen your faith, strengthen your relationships, and enhance your leadership.

On the flip side, neglecting essential habits—whether it's skipping prayer, procrastinating on important tasks, or failing to take care of your physical health—can lead to spiritual stagnation, stress, or burnout. Our habits, whether good or bad, shape the outcomes of our lives.

Jesus exemplified the power of habits in His leadership. Through consistent practices, He demonstrated how to live purposefully and lead effectively. Let's explore five key habits that defined His leadership and how we can integrate them into our own lives.

4. THE HABITS OF A LEADER

1. The Habit of Time Tracking

Time is one of the most valuable resources a leader has, yet it is often mismanaged or overlooked. Keeping a calendar or schedule helps you focus on what matters most and ensures you're prepared for critical moments.

Even Jesus, though He didn't carry a physical calendar, had a deep awareness of time and purpose. He often referenced the importance of timing in His ministry. For example, at the wedding in Cana, when His mother asked Him to address the lack of wine, He responded, *"My hour has not yet come"* (John 2:4). Yet, moments later, He performed His first miracle. Jesus knew exactly when to act and when to wait, demonstrating a profound respect for God's timing.

Ecclesiastes 3 reminds us that there is *"a time for everything, and a season for every activity under the heavens."* As leaders, we must respect the seasons of life and ministry, ensuring that our actions align with God's timing. Avoid the pitfall of doing the right thing at the wrong time. Cultivate the habit of tracking your time, setting priorities, and honoring the rhythms of life.

4. THE HABITS OF A LEADER

2. The Habit of Prioritizing

Leadership often means juggling multiple responsibilities, but not all tasks are created equal. The ability to prioritize—to put first things first—is a hallmark of effective leadership.

Jesus modeled this habit in Mark 1:35, where we see Him rising early in the morning to pray. Despite the demands of His ministry, He prioritized time with the Father above all else. This wasn't just a routine; it was a non-negotiable part of His day.

As leaders, we must ask ourselves: Are we busy, or are we purposely productive? There's a difference. Being busy often means doing many things, but productivity comes from focusing on the most important things. By prioritizing your tasks and commitments, you reduce stress, increase efficiency, and ensure that your energy is directed toward what truly matters.

3. The Habit of Solitude

In a world that often glorifies busyness, the practice of solitude can feel countercultural. Yet, solitude is essential for leaders who want to lead with clarity and purpose.

Jesus consistently withdrew to solitary places to pray and recharge. After His baptism, He spent 40 days in the wilderness, preparing for His ministry (Matthew 4:1-2). When He learned of John the Baptist's death, He sought solitude to grieve (Matthew 14:13). These moments of solitude weren't acts of isolation but opportunities to connect deeply with the Father, process emotions, and gain strength for the journey ahead.

4. THE HABITS OF A LEADER

For leaders, solitude provides a space to reflect, pray, and align our hearts with God's will. It's not about escaping responsibilities but about finding the strength to fulfill them.

4. The Habit of Building Relationships

While solitude is vital, leadership is ultimately about people. No leader can thrive in isolation. Relationships are the lifeblood of effective leadership, providing support, perspective, and encouragement.

Jesus surrounded Himself with a close-knit group of disciples. He traveled with them, taught them, and shared His life with them. Among the twelve, He had an even closer bond with Peter, James, and John. These relationships were not just functional; they were deeply personal. In His darkest hour, at Gethsemane, Jesus asked His disciples to stay with Him and pray (Matthew 26:36-38).

As leaders, we need trusted friends and colleagues who will stand with us in times of joy and grief, success and struggle. Building strong, authentic relationships requires effort, but the rewards are immeasurable.

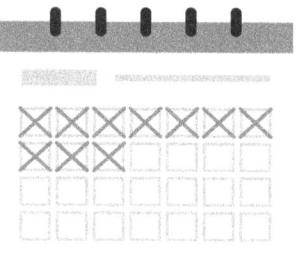

4. THE HABITS OF A LEADER

5. The Habit of Prayer

Prayer was the cornerstone of Jesus' life and ministry. From the beginning of His ministry—when He fasted and prayed for 40 days in the wilderness—to His final moments on the cross, Jesus demonstrated the importance of prayer.

Prayer is not just a spiritual discipline; it's a leadership strategy. It connects us to the source of wisdom, strength, and guidance. In Luke 5:16, we read, *"But Jesus often withdrew to lonely places and prayed."* This wasn't a last resort for Jesus; it was His first response.

As leaders, we must cultivate a habit of consistent, heartfelt prayer. Begin and end your day with prayer, seeking God's direction and thanking Him for His provision. Remember, prayer is not about perfection—it's about connection.

Conclusion: Habits as the Foundation of Leadership

Your habits are the building blocks of your leadership. They shape not only what you do but who you are. By cultivating habits like time tracking, prioritizing, solitude, relationships, and prayer, you can lead with greater clarity, purpose, and impact.

Leadership is not about perfection but about progression. Start small, be consistent, and trust that God will use your efforts to accomplish His will.

4. THE HABITS OF A LEADER

Reflection Questions:

What are some habits you currently practice that strengthen your leadership? Are there any habits you need to develop or refine?

How can you better prioritize your time to align with God's purpose for your life?

4. THE HABITS OF A LEADER

Reflection Questions:

Who are the key people in your life that support and challenge you as a leader?

How can you make prayer a more integral part of your daily routine?

CHAPTER 5

LEADING WITH OPENNESS AND BOLDNESS

5. LEADING WITH OPENNESS AND BOLDNESS

Leadership often conjures images of strength, confidence, and decisiveness. While these qualities are important, they are incomplete without openness and boldness. A leader who leads with openness fosters trust, cultivates deeper relationships, and creates a culture of authenticity. When paired with boldness—the courage to speak and act truthfully, even when it's uncomfortable—this combination transforms leadership from merely functional to profoundly impactful.

The Power of Vulnerability in Leadership

It's tempting to believe that leaders must have it all together. Many leaders feel the pressure to project an image of perfection, thinking that admitting mistakes or struggles will undermine their authority. But the truth is, vulnerability is a powerful leadership tool.

When leaders are willing to acknowledge their shortcomings and struggles, they humanize themselves. This doesn't make them weaker; it makes them relatable. Vulnerability creates connection because it reminds others that no one is exempt from challenges.

Consider the apostle Paul. In 2 Corinthians 12:9-10, he writes about a *"thorn in the flesh"*—a weakness he desperately wanted God to remove. Instead of delivering Paul from this weakness, God responded, *"My grace is sufficient for you, for my power is made perfect in weakness."* Paul's openness about his struggles didn't diminish his leadership; it deepened his reliance on God and inspired those he led to trust in God's grace.

5. LEADING WITH OPENNESS AND BOLDNESS

As a leader, it's okay to say, "I don't know," "I made a mistake," or "I'm struggling with this." These admissions don't undermine your credibility; they build trust and invite others to support you in ways that strengthen the entire team.

Honesty: The Foundation of Trust

Honesty is the bedrock of effective leadership. Without it, trust crumbles, and relationships falter. Leaders who are honest, even when the truth is difficult, demonstrate integrity and earn the respect of those they lead.

Jesus exemplified this in His interactions with the disciples. He never sugarcoated the challenges they would face. In John 16:33, He told them plainly, *"In this world you will have trouble. But take heart! I have overcome the world."* His honesty didn't discourage them; it prepared them.

As a leader, being honest means delivering both the good and the bad with clarity and compassion. Whether it's addressing poor performance, sharing difficult news, or admitting the limits of your own knowledge, honesty paves the way for growth and understanding.

5. LEADING WITH OPENNESS AND BOLDNESS

The Courage to Be Bold

Boldness in leadership is the willingness to speak and act with courage, even in the face of opposition, uncertainty, or fear. Boldness is not recklessness; it's rooted in conviction and guided by wisdom.

Jesus embodied boldness throughout His ministry. He boldly confronted injustice, challenged religious hypocrisy, and spoke truth to power—even when it put His life at risk. In John 2:13-17, we see Jesus driving out the money changers from the temple, declaring, *"Stop turning my Father's house into a market!"* This act was not just about cleansing a physical space; it was a bold statement about preserving the sacredness of God's house.

As leaders, we are often called to make bold decisions—standing up for what is right, even when it's unpopular, or taking risks that require faith. Boldness inspires those around you to act with courage and conviction.

Building Trust Through Openness and Boldness

Trust is the currency of leadership. Without it, progress stalls, and relationships erode. Trust is built when leaders are transparent about their intentions, consistent in their actions, and willing to engage in honest dialogue.

5. LEADING WITH OPENNESS AND BOLDNESS

One of the most profound ways to build trust is by admitting mistakes. When leaders take responsibility for their actions instead of deflecting blame, they model accountability and integrity. For example, in John 21, after Peter denied Jesus three times, Jesus didn't avoid the issue. Instead, He lovingly addressed it, asking Peter three times, *"Do you love me?"* This conversation not only restored Peter's confidence but also deepened the trust between him and Jesus.

Openness also involves listening. Leaders who actively seek feedback, value diverse perspectives, and create spaces where others feel safe to share their thoughts foster an environment of mutual respect and trust.

The Balance of Openness and Boldness

While openness invites connection, boldness drives action. Together, they create a balanced approach to leadership. A leader who is only open may risk appearing indecisive, while a leader who is only bold may come across as overbearing. The key is to integrate both qualities in a way that reflects humility and courage.

For example, when Nehemiah led the rebuilding of Jerusalem's walls, he exemplified both openness and boldness. He was transparent about the challenges ahead, sharing his vision and inviting others to join the effort (Nehemiah 2:17-18). At the same time, he boldly confronted opposition, reminding his team of God's power and purpose (Nehemiah 4:14). His leadership inspired unity, perseverance, and faith.

5. LEADING WITH OPENNESS AND BOLDNESS

Practical Steps to Lead with Openness and Boldness

1. **Practice Self-Awareness:** *Reflect on your own vulnerabilities, strengths, and areas for growth. Being self-aware allows you to lead authentically.*
2. **Admit Mistakes Quickly:** *When you make a mistake, own it. Apologize if necessary and focus on solutions rather than excuses.*
3. **Seek Feedback Regularly:** *Create opportunities for those you lead to share their thoughts and experiences. Ask questions like, "What can I do better?"*
4. **Speak the Truth in Love:** *Boldness doesn't mean being harsh. Frame difficult conversations with empathy and a desire to help the other person grow.*
5. **Trust God's Strength:** *Leading with openness and boldness requires reliance on God. Pray for wisdom, courage, and the ability to discern when to speak and when to listen.*

Conclusion: The Transformative Power of Openness and Boldness

Leadership that integrates openness and boldness reflects the heart of Christ. It shows that strength isn't about having all the answers but about being willing to learn, grow, and rely on God's grace.

When you lead with openness, you invite trust and connection. When you lead with boldness, you inspire action and courage. Together, these qualities create a leadership style that is authentic, effective, and deeply rooted in faith.

5. LEADING WITH OPENNESS AND BOLDNESS

Reflection Questions:

What fears or insecurities hold you back from being more open as a leader?

How do you balance being vulnerable with maintaining authority? Are there areas in your leadership where you need to be bolder?

5. LEADING WITH OPENNESS AND BOLDNESS

Reflection Questions:

How can you foster a culture of trust and transparency in your team?

What steps can you take this week to lead with greater openness and boldness?

CHAPTER 6

GREAT LEADERS LEAD THEMSELVES

6. GREAT LEADERS LEAD THEMSELVES

Leadership begins within. Before a leader can effectively guide others, they must first learn to lead themselves. This is a principle often overlooked, as leadership is frequently associated with influencing others, making decisions, and achieving goals. Yet, the foundation of all great leadership is self-leadership. Without self-discipline, self-awareness, and a commitment to personal growth, leaders risk burnout, poor decision-making, and losing the trust of those they lead.

Self-leadership is both a responsibility and a privilege. It's the acknowledgment that the most important person you will ever lead is yourself. This chapter will explore the biblical foundations of self-leadership and offer practical tools to help you grow into the leader God has called you to be.

Why Self-Leadership Matters

Imagine a shepherd who neglects to feed or care for themselves. They would soon lack the strength to tend to their flock, leaving the sheep vulnerable. In the same way, leaders who fail to lead themselves will eventually struggle to lead others effectively.

Proverbs 25:28 warns us, *"Like a city whose walls are broken through is a person who lacks self-control."* Without self-leadership, a leader becomes vulnerable to external pressures, internal weaknesses, and unwise decisions.

6. GREAT LEADERS LEAD THEMSELVES

Jesus, the ultimate example of leadership, consistently demonstrated self-leadership throughout His ministry. He prioritized prayer, rest, and intentional time with the Father, ensuring He was spiritually, emotionally, and physically equipped to fulfill His mission. If Jesus, the Son of God, modeled the importance of leading oneself, how much more should we?

The Building Blocks of Self-Leadership

1. Self-Awareness: Knowing Yourself

The first step in leading yourself is understanding yourself. Self-awareness involves recognizing your strengths, weaknesses, triggers, and blind spots. It's about being honest with yourself and seeking God's perspective on your identity and purpose.

David exemplified self-awareness in Psalm 139:23-24 when he prayed, *"Search me, God, and know my heart; test me and know my anxious thoughts. See if there is any offensive way in me, and lead me in the way everlasting."*

Practical Application:
- **Reflect:** Set aside time each week to reflect on your thoughts, actions, and decisions. Journaling can help you identify patterns and areas for growth.
- **Seek Feedback:** Invite trusted friends, mentors, or colleagues to share their perspectives on your leadership. Be open to both encouragement and constructive criticism.

6. GREAT LEADERS LEAD THEMSELVES

2. Self-Discipline: Mastering Your Actions

Leadership requires discipline. Great leaders don't wait for motivation; they take action even when it's difficult. Self-discipline enables you to stay focused, make wise choices, and persevere through challenges.

Paul writes in 1 Corinthians 9:27, *"I discipline my body and keep it under control, lest after preaching to others I myself should be disqualified."* A disciplined leader inspires others by their example and creates a foundation of trust and respect.

Practical Application:

- **Set Goals:** Establish clear, measurable goals for your personal and professional growth. Break them into actionable steps.

- **Create Routines:** Develop habits that align with your values and priorities, such as daily prayer, exercise, or time management practices.

- **Eliminate Distractions:** Identify what hinders your productivity or spiritual growth and take steps to minimize those distractions.

6. GREAT LEADERS LEAD THEMSELVES

3. Self-Care: Stewarding Your Well-Being

Self-care is not selfish; it's stewardship. God has entrusted you with your body, mind, and spirit, and it's your responsibility to care for them. Neglecting your well-being can lead to burnout, stress, and ineffective leadership.

Jesus demonstrated the importance of self-care when He withdrew to solitary places to rest and pray (Mark 6:31, Luke 5:16). These moments of renewal allowed Him to pour into others from a place of abundance rather than exhaustion.

Practical Application:

- **Prioritize Rest:** Ensure you're getting enough sleep and taking regular breaks. Honor the Sabbath as a day of rest and worship.

- **Invest in Your Health:** Eat nourishing foods, stay active, and manage stress through healthy outlets.

- **Nurture Your Spirit:** Spend time in prayer, worship, and Scripture to strengthen your relationship with God.

6. GREAT LEADERS LEAD THEMSELVES

4. Self-Accountability: Staying True to Your Values

Self-leadership involves holding yourself accountable to the standards and values you espouse. It's easy to set goals and make commitments, but follow-through requires intentionality.

Ecclesiastes 5:4-5 reminds us, *"When you make a vow to God, do not delay to fulfill it. He has no pleasure in fools; fulfill your vow. It is better not to make a vow than to make one and not fulfill it."*

Practical Application:

- **Use Accountability Tools:** Keep a journal, use apps, or create systems to track your progress and stay aligned with your commitments.

- **Partner with Others:** Share your goals with a trusted friend or mentor who can hold you accountable and encourage you along the way.

6. GREAT LEADERS LEAD THEMSELVES

5. Self-Inspiration: Leading with Vision

Great leaders inspire themselves before inspiring others. This means staying connected to your "why"—your God-given purpose and vision. When you lead yourself with a sense of mission, you inspire others to do the same.

Hebrews 12:1-2 encourages us to *"run with perseverance the race marked out for us, fixing our eyes on Jesus, the pioneer and perfecter of faith."* Staying focused on Christ helps us maintain clarity and motivation, even in challenging seasons.

Practical Application:

- **Revisit Your Vision:** Regularly remind yourself of your purpose and calling. Write it down and keep it somewhere visible.

- **Celebrate Wins:** Acknowledge and celebrate progress, no matter how small. Gratitude fuels perseverance.

- **Stay Inspired:** Read books, listen to sermons or podcasts, and surround yourself with people who encourage and challenge you.

6. GREAT LEADERS LEAD THEMSELVES

The Ripple Effect of Self-Leadership

When leaders prioritize self-leadership, they not only grow personally but also create a positive ripple effect on those they lead. A well-led leader models integrity, resilience, and humility, inspiring others to pursue their own growth.

Consider Nehemiah, who led the rebuilding of Jerusalem's walls. Before rallying others, he spent time in prayer, fasting, and planning (Nehemiah 1:4-11). His commitment to self-leadership equipped him to face opposition and accomplish God's vision.

Conclusion: Leadership Begins with You

Leading yourself is not a one-time event; it's a lifelong journey of growth, discipline, and dependence on God. As you lead yourself well, you position yourself to lead others with authenticity and effectiveness.

Great leaders don't wait for external validation or motivation—they take ownership of their development and trust God to guide their steps. Remember, the most significant influence you'll ever have begins with how you lead your own life.

6. GREAT LEADERS LEAD THEMSELVES

Reflection Questions:

In what areas of your life do you struggle with self-leadership?

How can you become more self-aware of your strengths and weaknesses?

6. GREAT LEADERS LEAD THEMSELVES

Reflection Questions:

What daily habits or routines could you implement to strengthen your self-leadership?

How does your relationship with God influence your ability to lead yourself?

87

CONCLUSION

Conclusion

Becoming the Leader God Has Called You to Be

As we come to the close of this journey through leadership, let's pause to reflect on the truths we've explored together. Leadership, as modeled by Jesus, is not about position or power—it's about influence, character, and purpose. It's about living out your God-given calling in a way that inspires and equips others to do the same.

Throughout this book, we've unpacked the foundational principles of leading like Jesus. From the humility to serve others to the courage to embrace accountability, the habits of self-leadership, and the vulnerability that builds trust, each chapter has revealed that leadership is less about outward actions and more about inward transformation.

But where do we go from here? How do we take these principles and make them a tangible part of our daily lives?

This concluding chapter will tie together the lessons we've learned, offer encouragement for the journey ahead, and provide practical next steps to help you grow as the leader God has called you to be.

Looking Back: The Foundation of Leadership

The Heart of Leadership

At the core of leadership is humility. Jesus taught us that to lead is to serve. His life was a testament to this truth, as He washed His disciples' feet and laid down His life for us. Leadership begins with a heart that prioritizes others over self and seeks to glorify God above all else.

The Accountability of Leadership

Accountability reminds us that we are not meant to lead alone. Great leaders are willing to be held accountable—not out of fear but out of a desire to grow and stay aligned with their mission. When we surround ourselves with wise counsel and invite others to speak into our lives, we strengthen our character and effectiveness.

The Habits of Leadership

Habits shape our future. As we learned from Jesus' example, prioritizing time with God, managing our time well, and nurturing relationships are essential disciplines of effective leadership. These habits enable us to lead from a place of strength and alignment with God's will.

The Vulnerability of Leadership

Openness and honesty build trust. Great leaders are not afraid to admit their shortcomings or seek forgiveness. When we lead with vulnerability, we model the grace and redemption of Christ, creating a culture of authenticity and growth.

Leading Yourself First

Self-leadership is the foundation upon which all other leadership is built. When we take responsibility for our growth, practice self-discipline, and prioritize our well-being, we honor God and equip ourselves to lead others well.

Conclusion

Looking Ahead: Embracing the Call to Lead
As you move forward, consider the following steps to solidify what you've learned and continue growing as a leader:

1. Return to the Source
Leadership is a divine calling, and your strength to lead comes from God. Make it a priority to spend time in His presence daily. Prayer, Scripture, and worship are not optional for a Christian leader—they are the lifeblood of your leadership.

Practical Tip: Begin each day by asking God for wisdom, strength, and guidance. James 1:5 promises, "If any of you lacks wisdom, you should ask God, who gives generously to all without finding fault, and it will be given to you."

2. Reflect and Reassess
Take time to evaluate your leadership journey regularly. What areas are you thriving in? Where do you need to grow? Reflection helps you stay aligned with God's purpose and allows you to course-correct when needed.

Practical Tip: Schedule a quarterly "leadership check-in" with yourself or a mentor. Use this time to reflect on your progress, celebrate wins, and set new goals.

Conclusion

3. Build Your Team
Leadership is not a solo endeavor. Identify people who can support, challenge, and encourage you. This could include mentors, accountability partners, or a small group of trusted friends.

Practical Tip: Consider forming a leadership cohort—a small group of peers who meet regularly to share insights, pray for one another, and offer feedback.

4. Lead by Example
The most powerful way to lead is through your actions. People are watching how you respond to challenges, handle success, and treat others. Strive to be a reflection of Christ in all you do.

Practical Tip: Ask yourself daily, "What would Jesus do in my situation?" Then act accordingly.

5. Commit to Lifelong Growth
Leadership is a journey, not a destination. Stay curious, remain teachable, and be open to new opportunities for growth. Remember, even the greatest leaders are still growing.

Practical Tip: Dedicate time each month to learning—whether through reading books, attending workshops, or seeking feedback from others.

Conclusion

Encouragement for the Journey

As you step into your role as a leader, remember that God doesn't call the equipped; He equips the called. You don't have to be perfect to lead; you just need to be willing. Trust that God will provide the wisdom, strength, and grace you need for every challenge you face.

Philippians 1:6 reminds us, "Being confident of this, that he who began a good work in you will carry it on to completion until the day of Christ Jesus." God is faithful to complete the work He has started in you.

You've been called to lead, and you've been equipped with the tools to do so. Now it's time to step out in faith, embrace the journey, and lead like Jesus. Your impact can ripple through lives, families, communities, and generations. Lead boldly, lead humbly, and lead well.

Closing Prayer

Heavenly Father,

Thank You for the privilege of leadership and the opportunity to serve others for Your glory. Help us to lead with humility, courage, and wisdom. Strengthen our hearts, sharpen our minds, and guide our steps as we seek to reflect Jesus in all we do. May our leadership bring honor to Your name and draw others closer to You. In Jesus' name, we pray. Amen.

CONCLUSION

Reflection Questions:

Which leadership principle from this book resonated with you the most, and why?

What practical steps will you take to grow in your leadership over the next month?

CONCLUSION

Reflection Questions:

Who can you invite into your leadership journey to support and hold you accountable?

How can you rely on God more fully in your leadership?

NEXT STEPS ON YOUR JOURNEY

We believe that your journey with God doesn't end here—it's just the beginning! Here are a few ways you can take the next step:

1. Strengthen Your Faith
   - Daily Devotions: Spend time with God each day. Reflect on His Word and pray for guidance.
   - Bible Study Groups: Join or start a small group to grow in community and deepen your understanding of Scripture.
2. Stay Connected
   - Follow us on Facebook for encouragement, updates, and community.
   - Subscribe to our Newsletter for exclusive devotionals, resources, and upcoming events.
3. Take Action
   - Get Involved: Serve your local community or church.
   - Give Back: Consider supporting our ongoing mission in Egypt.
4. Reach Out
   - Have questions, need prayer, or want to share your story? We'd love to hear from you!
     - Email: EgyptProject@Proton.me
     - Visit: www.EgyptProject.org
5. Go Deeper
   - Explore our additional resources, including books, podcasts, and study guides designed to help you grow in faith and purpose.

Your Journey Matters

Whether you're taking your first step toward faith or looking to deepen your walk with God, remember this: you're never alone. God is with you, and so are we.

Let us know how we can support you—your journey is important to us!

Connect With Us. We're here to support and encourage you!

The Shepherd's Guide: Leadership Lessons from the Greatest Leader
Copyright © 2025 Relentless Publications

All rights reserved.
No part of this publication may be reproduced, distributed, or transmitted in any form or by any means, including photocopying, recording, or other electronic or mechanical methods, without the prior written permission of the publisher, except in the case of brief quotations embodied in critical reviews and certain other noncommercial uses permitted by copyright law.

ISBN: 978-1-960296-06-1 (Paperback)

Any references to historical events, real people, or real places are used fictitiously. Names, characters, and places are products of the author's imagination.

This book is not intended to diagnose, treat, cure, or prevent any disease.
DISCLAIMER: THIS BOOK DOES NOT PROVIDE MEDICAL OR THERAPEUTIC ADVICE.
The information, including but not limited to, text, graphics, images and other material contained are for informational purposes only. No material is intended to be a substitute for professional medical advice, diagnosis or treatment. Always seek the advice of your physician or other qualified health care provider with any questions you may have regarding a medical condition or treatment and before undertaking a new health care regimen, and never disregard professional medical advice or delay in seeking it because of something you have read herewith.

Scripture quotations are taken from: New American Standard Bible (NASB), © 1960, 1977, 1995 by the Lockman Foundation. The New King James Version of the Bible (KJV). The New King James Bible (NKJV ®), copyright © 1982 by Thomas Nelson, Inc. The Holy Bible, English Standard Version TM (ESV) copyright 2001 by Crossway Bibles, a division of Good News Publishers. All rights reserved. New International Reader's Version (NIRV) copyright © 1996, 1998 by International Bible Society. All rights reserved worldwide. The Holy Bible, New International Version (NIV). Copyright © 1973, 1978, 1984, International Bible Society. Used by permission. New Living Translation. Copyright © 1996, 2004, 2015 by Tyndale House Foundation. Used by permission of Tyndale House Ministries, Carol Stream, Illinois 60188. All rights reserved.

Front cover image by public domain www.pexels.com.

Book design by Relentless Publications, Inc.

Printed by Relentless Publications, Inc., in the United States of America.

First printing edition 2025

www.EgyptProject.org
www.Soul-CareCoaching.com
www.RelentlessLiving.com
www.MyMarriageIntensive.com
www.RelationshipCohort.com
www.DianaAsaad.com

www.ingramcontent.com/pod-product-compliance
Lightning Source LLC
Chambersburg PA
CBHW060845050426
42453CB00008B/844